Amusement Parks

Perimeter and Area

Dianne Irving

Publishing Credits

Editor
Sara Johnson

Editorial Director
Dona Herweck Rice

Editor-in-Chief
Sharon Coan, M.S.Ed.

Creative Director
Lee Aucoin

Publisher
Rachelle Cracchiolo, M.S.Ed.

Image Credits

Teacher Created Materials

5301 Oceanus Drive
Huntington Beach, CA 92649-1030
http://www.tcmpub.com
ISBN 978-0-7439-0918-1
© 2009 Teacher Created Materials, Inc.
Made in China
Nordica.032016.CA21600284

Table of Contents

Amusement Parks

Amusement parks are lots of fun. They have rides, games, and other entertainment. There are different kinds of amusement parks. Some are small with only a few rides. Some are huge and have themes. Each park is carefully planned to fit a certain **area**.

The Ferris wheel is a popular ride all around the world. The first Ferris wheel was built in Chicago in 1893.

This amusement park has many amazing rides.

Designers (duh-ZINE-erz) plan buildings and gardens to make theme parks look good. Theme parks are designed to give visitors lots of fun and also to keep them safe. Theme parks must be carefully planned so that all the **attractions** (uh-TRAK-shuhns) will fit. Each of these attractions must be carefully designed, too.

Long-lasting Fun

The oldest amusement park in the world is in Denmark. People originally visited Bakken to drink its natural spring water more than 400 years ago. Today, this park has rides, performers, and places for eating.

History of Amusement Parks

The first amusement parks began in Europe in the 1500s. They were called pleasure gardens. This is because there were many attractions that made people happy. There was music, games, and rides. There were also flower gardens, fountains, and stage shows. In the 1600s, many of the pleasure gardens shut down.

People liked going to Coney Island because there were fun attractions and they could also swim.

Amusement parks were not popular again until the 1800s. Parks started to make roller coasters. The first roller coaster in the United States was built in Coney Island. It opened in 1884.

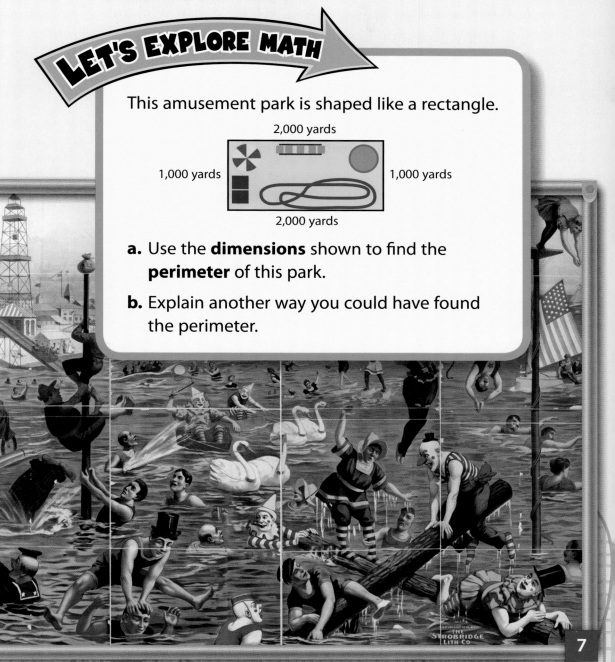

LET'S EXPLORE MATH

This amusement park is shaped like a rectangle.

2,000 yards

1,000 yards   1,000 yards

2,000 yards

a. Use the **dimensions** shown to find the **perimeter** of this park.

b. Explain another way you could have found the perimeter.

Many of the first roller coasters were made of wood. It was risky to go upside down on wooden coasters. So, they had many quick drops and sharp turns. Later, **steel** was used to make roller coasters. These coasters were safer. They could go upside down. Roller coasters made people enjoy amusement parks again.

This wooden roller coaster looks very different from the roller coasters at amusement parks today.

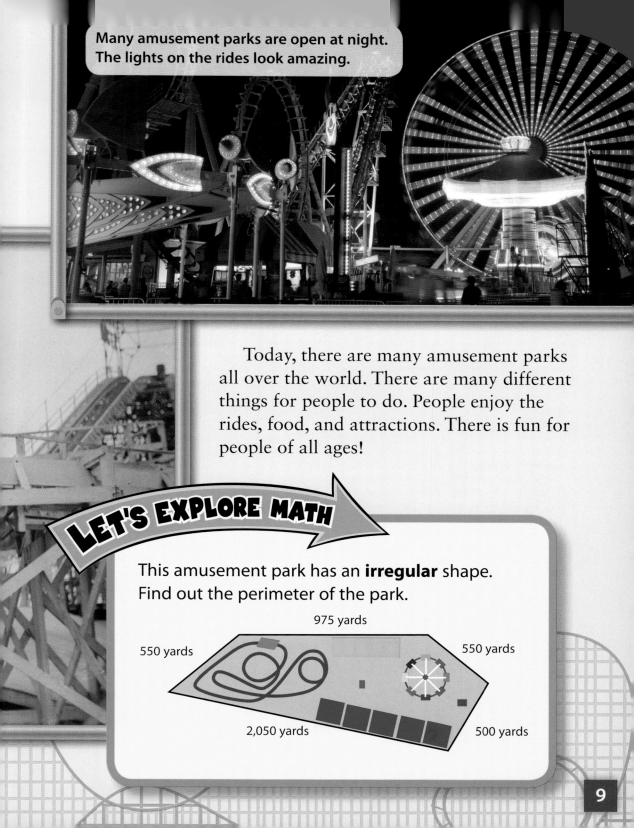

Many amusement parks are open at night.
The lights on the rides look amazing.

Today, there are many amusement parks all over the world. There are many different things for people to do. People enjoy the rides, food, and attractions. There is fun for people of all ages!

LET'S EXPLORE MATH

This amusement park has an **irregular** shape. Find out the perimeter of the park.

975 yards

550 yards

550 yards

2,050 yards

500 yards

Amusement Park Rides

Roller coasters

Roller coasters can fit around the perimeter of a park. They can even go over the top of other rides and attractions. The loops in the track save space, too. By carefully planning the roller coaster track, the space in the amusement park can be used well.

This roller coaster in Hong Kong goes over the lush rainforest below.

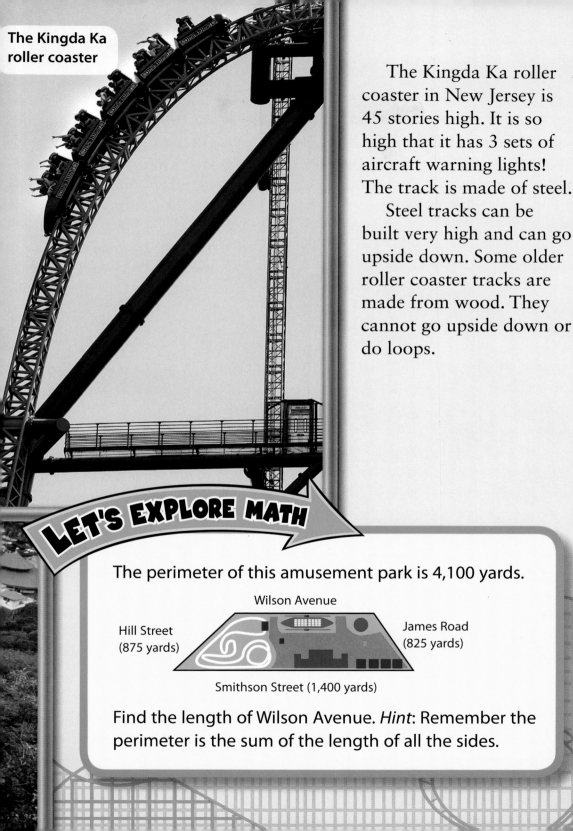

The Kingda Ka roller coaster

The Kingda Ka roller coaster in New Jersey is 45 stories high. It is so high that it has 3 sets of aircraft warning lights! The track is made of steel.

Steel tracks can be built very high and can go upside down. Some older roller coaster tracks are made from wood. They cannot go upside down or do loops.

LET'S EXPLORE MATH

The perimeter of this amusement park is 4,100 yards.

Wilson Avenue

Hill Street (875 yards)

James Road (825 yards)

Smithson Street (1,400 yards)

Find the length of Wilson Avenue. *Hint*: Remember the perimeter is the sum of the length of all the sides.

This roller coaster in Blackpool, England, is a long ride that was designed to fit into a short space. On the ground, the length of the space taken up by the roller coaster is only 52 feet (15.8 m). But if you stretched out the whole track, it would be 5,463 feet (1.6 km) long!

The roller coaster has many twists and dips.

Roller Coaster Record
In 2000, Richard Rodriguez rode a roller coaster for 2,000 hours without stopping. He traveled 12,000 miles (over 19,000 km).

This roller coaster took more than 3 years to build. Any rides that were in the way of the new track were taken down. The **foundations** (fown-DAY-shuhns) were built, and then the rest of the roller coaster was made from about 2,900 tons (2,630 t) of steel. More than 60,000 bolts were used to put the ride together.

The amusement park in Blackpool, England, dates back to 1896.

LET'S EXPLORE MATH

To find the area of a rectangle, we can multiply the length by the width. If the length measurements are in meters, the area measurement is in square meters (m^2). If the length measurements are in yards, the area measurement is in square yards ($yd.^2$).

A roller coaster takes up a space that is 50 meters long and 25 meters wide. What is the area of the space the roller coaster takes up?

Dark Rides

A dark ride is a ride in which visitors travel in a small **carriage** in the dark. The ride takes place inside a building. It is often designed to scare visitors. Some dark rides travel very fast. Visitors feel a thrill from the speed and the dark. A popular dark ride at many amusement parks is the ghost train ride.

Ghost train

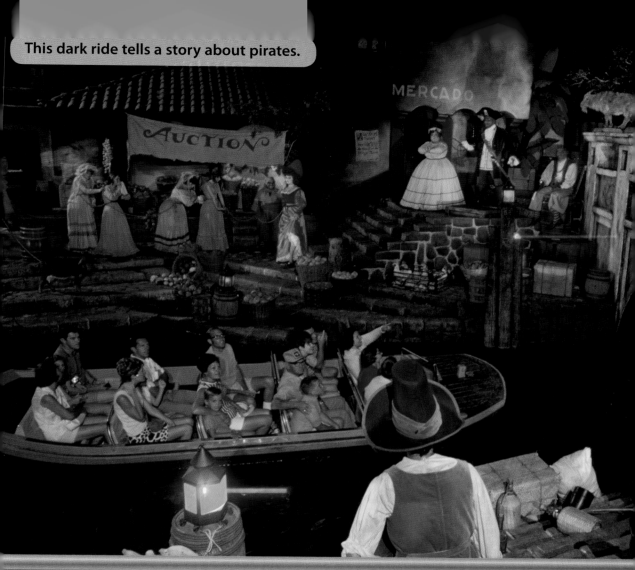

This dark ride tells a story about pirates.

Other dark rides travel slowly. They are designed to tell a story to visitors as the ride progresses. The rides may have sound effects or music. This can help enhance the story.

Sometimes these rides have more then one level. The carriage or boat may suddenly drop or rise as the ride goes along.

Children's Rides

Many rides for children, such as the carousel (KARE-uh-sell), do not need a big area. Often the rides for small children are built close together, so it is easy for them to get to each ride.

A carousel

In California, the Goliath Jr. roller coaster was built especially for children. It is based on a roller coaster for adults that travels as high as 255 feet (77.7 m). But the children's roller coaster only travels as high as 10 feet (3 m).

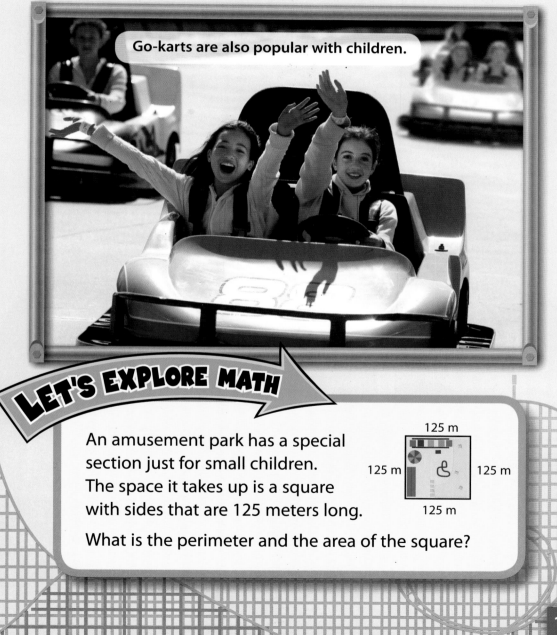

Go-karts are also popular with children.

LET'S EXPLORE MATH

An amusement park has a special section just for small children. The space it takes up is a square with sides that are 125 meters long.

125 m
125 m
125 m
125 m

What is the perimeter and the area of the square?

Small children also like the tilt-a-whirl ride. It has carriages that spin around. The carriages are on a platform that moves. As the platform moves, the carriages spin in different directions.

This kind of spinning ride was first made in the 1920s. The platform is made from steel. The carriages are made from **fiberglass**. The steps and handrails are made from **aluminium** (ah-LOO-mihn-uhm).

Some spinning rides are more than 50 years old. They are still being used today.

People sit in swings for this spinning ride.

LET'S EXPLORE MATH

Most rides need barriers around them to keep the public safe. One ride has a safety fence around it that forms a square. The perimeter of the square is 200 yards.

a. What is the length of each side of the square?

b. What is the area of the ride?

Water Parks

Water parks are amusement parks that have attractions such as waterslides and wave pools. One of the largest water parks in the United States is in Wisconsin. It has 45 waterslides, 2 rivers, and 2 huge wave pools. Two of the waterslides are 10 stories tall! But people take less than 5 seconds to slide down them.

Water Park Measurements
Area: 70 acres (28.3 ha)

LET'S EXPLORE MATH

The water park in Miyazaki, Japan, is shaped like a rectangle. One side is 300 meters long and the other side is 100 meters long.

a. What is the perimeter of the water park?

b. What is the area of the water park?

Water parks can be built indoors or outdoors. The water park in Japan is the largest indoor water park in the world. The dome has a roof that slides open and shut. Inside the dome, there is a beach with sand and an **artificial** (ar-tuh-FISH-uhl) ocean that has waves.

Water Park Measurements
Height: 124 feet (37.7 m)
Length: 984 feet (300 m)
Width: 328 feet (100 m)

At a water park in Texas, the Master Blaster ride starts at the top of a tower. Visitors travel in boats. The boats drop down 3 levels and then they are lifted back up. **Jets** of water move the boats around on a water course that is 1,000 feet (304.8 m) long.

Many water parks have "lazy rivers." These rivers have a gentle **current**. People can sit in tubes and float along the river.

There are also "wave rivers." These rivers use waves made by a machine to carry people along the river. The rivers are oftened designed to flow around the perimeter of the park, so they are very long. They can even be designed to flow around attractions.

Long Ride
The Raging River ride in Texas is the world's longest lazy river ride. It is 1 mile (1.6 km) long.

When an amusement park is being planned, designers think about how people are going to get around the park. At many of the big theme parks, there are trains to help people get around. But all parks need good walking paths, too.

People walk around an amusement park.

LET'S EXPLORE MATH

An amusement park has 4 different rides. Each ride has a safety fence. What is the total length of each of the fences around the rides?

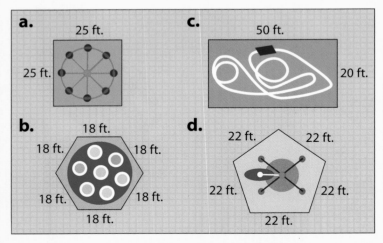

a.

25 ft.

25 ft.

b.

18 ft.

18 ft.   18 ft.

18 ft.   18 ft.

18 ft.

c.

50 ft.

20 ft.

d.

22 ft.   22 ft.

22 ft.   22 ft.

22 ft.

e. What is the total length of all the fences around the rides?

People must also have enough room to line up for the rides. Often, visitors can watch the ride while they wait. This can make them even more excited about taking the ride!

Shopping for an Amusement Park?

In Minnesota, there is an amusement park in the middle of a shopping mall. The park is set on 7 acres (2.8 ha). Even though it is indoors, the park has 2 roller coasters.

25

Planning for Fun

All amusement parks and rides need careful planning and measuring. Each ride must have just the right amount of space so that visitors are kept safe. With the right plans and measurements, designers can get as many rides as possible into an amusement park.

Too Much Fun

Dorothea Spohler-Claussen holds the world record for the most visits to amusement parks. She made 1,108 visits to 149 different parks in 12 countries. She did this between 1976 and 2005.

This large amusement park has both rides and water attractions.

New rides are being designed and built all the time. Sometimes, rides are taken down and replaced with new ones. Often, amusement parks put in more and more rides. They just keep getting bigger over time. Amusement parks are well planned, so you can plan to have fun!

PROBLEM-SOLVING ACTIVITY

Carnival Fun

Chen and Natasha are planning a school carnival. Below is a plan of where everything can be found at the carnival. On their plan, each small square is 5 yards x 5 yards.

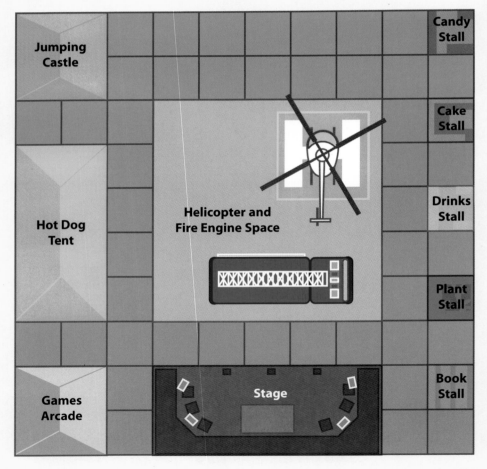

Solve It!

a. The space for the helicopter and fire engine needs to be fenced off with rope. How many yards of rope are needed?

b. Find the dimensions of the stage. Then calculate the area of the stage.

c. Find the total area of the 5 small stalls.

d. Chen and Natasha can fit 4 sets of tables and chairs in 25 square yards. Calculate how many sets of tables and chairs they could fit in half the area of the hot dog tent.

Use the steps below to help you work out your answers.

Step 1: Find the perimeter of the helicopter and fire engine space.

Step 2: Find the length and width of the stage. Then figure out the area.

Step 3: Figure out the area of each of the stalls. Then add the areas.

Step 4: Figure out the area of the hot dog tent. Halve the area. Then figure out how many sets of tables and chairs can fit into that area.

Glossary

aluminum—a metal that is very light and flexible

area—the space inside a particular shape or place

artificial—fake, not real

attractions—things that people want to see or visit

carriage—a vehicle used for carrying people

current—the movement or flow of water

designers—people who draw plans for objects or buildings

dimensions—size or measurements

fiberglass—a strong but light material that is made from glass fibers

foundations—the bases of buildings

irregular—unusual, not a regular shape

jets—nozzles through which a rush of water is pushed through a narrow opening

perimeter—the distance around the edge of a shape or space

steel—a very strong metal

Index

Let's Explore Math

Page 7:
a. Perimeter: 2,000 yds. + 1,000 yds.
   + 2,000 yds. + 1,000 yds.
   = 6,000 yards
b. Answers will vary.

Page 9:
a. Perimeter: 550 yds. + 975 yds.
   + 550 yds. + 500 yds. + 2,050 yds.
   = 4,625 yards

Page 11:
875 yds. + 1,400 yds. + 825 yds.
= 3,100 yards
Perimeter = 4,100 yards
4,100 yds. − 3,100 yds. = 1,000 yds.
Wilson Avenue = 1,000 yards

Page 13:
50 m × 25 m = 1,250 square meters (m^2)

Page 17:
Perimeter: 125 m + 125 m + 125 m
+ 125 m = 500 m
or 125 m × 4 = 500 m
Area: 125 m × 125 m
= 15,625 square meters (m^2)

Page 19:
a. Each side is 50 yards long
   50 yds. + 50 yds. + 50 yds. + 50 yds.
   = 200 yards
b. 50 yds. × 50 yds.
   = 2,500 square yards (yds.^{2})

Page 20:
a. Perimeter: 300 m + 100 m + 300 m
   + 100 m = 800 m
b. Area: 300 m × 100 m
   = 30,000 square meters (m^2)

Page 24:
a. 25 ft. × 4 = 100 ft. or
   25 ft. + 25 ft. + 25 ft. + 25 ft. = 100 ft.
b. 18 ft. × 6 = 108 ft. or
   18 ft. + 18 ft. +18 ft. + 18 ft. + 18 ft.
   + 18 ft. = 108 ft.
c. 50 ft. + 20 ft. + 50 ft. + 20 ft. = 140 ft.
d. 22 ft. × 5 = 110 ft. or
   22 ft. + 22 ft. + 22 ft. + 22 ft. + 22 ft.
   = 110 ft.
e. Total length of fences needed:
   100 ft. + 140 ft. + 108 ft. + 110 ft.
   = 458 ft.

Problem-Solving Activity

a. Perimeter of helicopter and fire engine space: 25 yds. × 4 = 100 yds.
b. Stage dimensions: 25 yds. long and 10 yds. wide.
   Area of stage: 25 yds. × 10 yds. = 250 yds.^{2}
c. Total area: 25 yds.^{2} + 25 yds.^{2} + 25 yds.^{2} + 25 yds.^{2} + 25 yds.^{2} = 125 yds.^{2}
d. Area = 20 yds. × 10 yds. = 200 yds.^{2}
   $\frac{1}{2}$ of 200 yds.^{2} = 100 yds.^{2}
   100 yds.^{2} ÷ 25 yds.^{2} = 4
   4 sets of tables and chairs × 4 = 16 sets of tables and chairs